JEWISH CUSTOMS AND TRADITIONS

Exhibition Guide

P9-CBR-628

ŽIDOVSKÉ
MUZEUM
PRAHA

Torah Scroll

FESTIVALS,
THE SYNAGOGUE
AND THE COURSE
OF LIFE

Jewish Customs and Traditions

(Exhibition Guide)

Alexandr Putík – Eva Kosáková
Dana Cabanová

THE JEWISH MUSEUM
IN PRAGUE

PRAGUE 1998

JEWISH CUSTOMS AND TRADITIONS
FESTIVALS, THE SYNAGOGUE
AND THE COURSE OF LIFE

***Permanent Exhibition
in the Klausen Synagogue
and the Ceremonial Hall
of the Burial Society***

The first part of the exhibition was opened
in the Main Hall of the Klausen Synagogue
on 30th April 1996,
the second part in the Gallery
of the Klausen Synagogue
and in the Ceremonial Hall
on 18th March 1998

Curators of the Exhibition:
PhDr. Alexandr Putík *(exhibition concept, texts)*
PhDr. Eva Kosáková *(selection of exhibits)*

Curators of Collections:
Mgr. Michaela Hájková
(collection of paintings and graphic art)
PhDr. Ludmila Kybalová, CSc
(collection of textiles)
Jaroslav Kuntoš
(collection of metal artefacts)
Mgr. Olga Sixtová
(collection of manuscripts and old prints)
Vlastimila Hamáčková
*(archives of the Jewish
communities)*

Protection of Architectural Monuments:
PhDr. Arno Pařík
*(supervision of the reconstruction
of the Klausen Synagogue and the Ceremonial Hall)*

Museum Restorers:
Pavel Veselý
Martina Jarešová
Helena Votočková
Veronika Nauschová

Architects:
akad. arch. Martin Vopálka
akad. arch. Jana Heroutová

Implementation:
ATYP EXPO,
BV Arrangement,
Pavel Břach

Main Hall of the Klausen Synagogue

1) Curtain. Velvet embroidered with metallic and silk threads, Prague 1695. /Donated by David Oppenheim and his wife Gnendele to the Old-New Synagogue/

JUDAISM
AND ITS SOURCES

Judaism is the oldest monotheist religion based on faith in God the Creator and Ruler of the World. The source of the Jewish faith is in the *Torah* (Hebrew teaching) which covers a set of rules and principles that come from God's revelation on Mount Sinai. In the broadest sense the Torah is a summation of two mutually linked parts – the written and the oral. The written Torah is the Hebrew Bible (in the Christian tradition it is called the Old Testament). The most customary term for the Hebrew Bible is *Tanakh*. The Hebrew canon is divided into three basic parts – the Torah (in the narrow sense of the word), the Prophets and the Writings. The greatest respect is given to the Torah – the Five Books of Moses also known as *Hamisha Humshei Torah* or the Pentateuch. The Books of Moses are not only a dramatic history. An integral part of them are the 613 precepts (*mitzvot*) which lay down the rules of religious law, rites and morality. The most honoured place among them belongs to the ethical basis of European civilisation – the Decalogue or the Ten Commandments. The Books contained in the Prophets bear witness to the life and dicta of men chosen to communicate God's will to the people. This section includes the Books of Joshua, Judges, Samuel, Kings, Isaiah, Jeremiah, Ezekiel and the Twelve Minor Prophets. The third part of the canon, the Writings, includes liturgical poetry, wise sayings and history. This part contains the Books of Psalms, Proverbs, Job, Song of Songs, Ruth, Lamentations of Jeremiah, Ecclesiastes and Esther, Daniel, Ezra and Nehemiah and the Chronicles. The oral Torah, which explains and develops the written Torah, covers two areas – halakhah and aggadah. *Halakhah* (walking) is a summary of religious law. *Aggadah* (narration) in contrast is devoted mainly to ethical and philosophical questions elucidated by stories and parables. The teaching of halakhah, retained in the form of discussions by scholars, was classified and edited by the Patriarch Judah ha-Nasi ca. 200 C.E. His Hebrew written work, *Mishnah* (repetition, teaching), contains six divisions which are further divided into tractates. The Mishnah formed the starting point for examinations by scholars of succeeding generations. Their discussions about halakhic, as well as haggadic questions, are recorded in Aramaic-written *Gemarah* (completion). The Mishnah and Gemarah together form the *Talmud*. This work exists in two versions: the Jerusalem Talmud concluded in the 4th century, and the Babylonian Talmud completed in the 5th century. Another way of retaining the oral Torah is through *midrash* (investigation), which takes the form of explanation of the individual books of the Bible.

JEWISH CALENDAR

The Jewish calendar is lunar-solar – the months are counted according to the lunar cycle, the years according to the solar cycle. The length of the months corresponds roughly to the real length of time that it takes the Moon to orbit the Earth. Because this occurs approximately every 29.5 days a month (Heb. *hodesh*) is either 29 or 30 days. The New Month, *Rosh Hodesh*, begins with the new moon – the first appearance of the crescent. The beginning of the month was originally proclaimed on the basis of direct observation of the Moon. From the middle of the 4th century, the months were determined by a stable calendar put together on the basis of precise chronological calculations. The months are reckoned from the first spring month known as *Nissan*. It is followed by *Iyyar, Sivan, Tammuz, Av, Elul, Tishri, Heshvan, Kislev, Tevet, Shevat* and *Adar*. The years, according to the era of the creation of the world, begin with the first day of the month of Tishri. The lunar year consists of twelve cycles of the Moon which on average is 11 days shorter than the solar year. The difference equals out roughly once in two or three years by adding a 13th month *Vaadar* or *Adar Sheni* (i.e. the se-

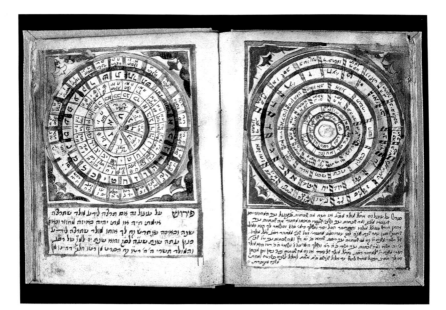

cond Adar). This adjustment (i.e., intercalation) is necessary if Nissan is to fall at the beginning of spring. For the rhythm of religious life the period of seven days, or the week (*shavuah*), is of vital importance. The first day of the Jewish calendar is Sunday, the seventh is Saturday – the Sabbath. The day begins in the evening (at the end of twilight). That is why, for example, the Sabbath (Saturday) starts Friday evening.

2) Eliezer ben Jacob Bellin, Evronot (Intercalations of Months). Manuscript on paper, ink, tempera, Central Europe, first half of the 18th century. /Chronological handbook for arranging calendars/

The order of Jewish divine service, determined by the alternation of day and night, prescribes three main daily prayers: morning (*Shaharit*), afternoon (*Minhah*), and evening (*Maariv*). The texts of the prayers for weekdays and the Sabbath are to be found in the prayer book known as *Siddur* (order). In the Jewish concept of divine services, prayers are regarded as a substitute for sacrifices, offered at one time in the Temple of Jerusalem. In the liturgy the greatest significance is given to two units. The first is *Shema Yisrael*, the second *Shemoneh Esreh*. The core of *Shema Yisrael* is made up of three parts from the Torah (Deuteronomy 6, 4-9; 11, 13-21; Numbers 15, 37-41) which begin with a declaration of faith: "Hear, O Israel! The Lord is our God, the Lord is One." The prayer *Shemoneh Esreh* (Eighteen Blessings), is also known as *Amidah* (a prayer recited while standing). Besides professing the almightiness and holiness of God of Patriarchs and thanks for performing miracles, it also expresses the most varied supplications which reflect universal and national concerns and aspirations as well as everyday needs. Whereas Shema Yisrael is said only in the morning and evening, Amidah is part of all three daily prayers. The Shema section in the morning divine service is preceded by the liturgical text known as *Pesuke de-Zimrah* (the Verses of Praise), in which the most important place is given to Psalms. All the above-mentioned parts of the liturgy are also

3) Tefillot Yisrael. Modlitby Israelitůw (Prayers of Israelites). Vienna, 1847. /The first Siddur with a translation into Czech/

said on the Sabbath and holidays. Worshippers pray, if possible, during public synagogue divine service. Most prayers can be said at home during individual services. Public services require the presence of a quorum of at least ten adult men (*minyan*).

TALLIT, TEFILLIN, HEAD COVERINGS

A characteristic feature of Jewish morning prayer is the use of prayer shawls and phylacteries. Whereas the shawl (*tallit*) is worn by men on weekdays and also on the Sabbath and holidays, phylacteries (*tefillin*) are tied only on weekdays. Women do not use the tallit or the tefillin. Both customs come from the commandments contained in the prayer *Shema Yisrael*. Relating to the tefillin are the words: "You shall love the Lord your God with all your heart and with all your soul and with all your

4) Large Tallit. Wool, Bohemia, early 20th century. Tefillin for the Head and Arm. Leather, Bohemia, late 19th century. /From the property of the Klausen Synagogue/

5) Tefillin Cases. Engraved silver, Russia, second half of the 19th century

6) Yarmulkah. Velvet embroidered with metallic threads, Bohemia, late 19th century

might. And these words which I command you this day shall be in your heart... You shall bind them as a sign on your hand, and they shall be frontlets between your eyes" (Deuteronomy 6, 5-8). The purpose of wearing the tallit comes from the verses: "...and they shall make for themselves fringes on the corners of their garments throughout their generations, and they shall attach a cord of blue to the fringe at each corner. That shall be your fringe, look at it so that you will recall all the commandments of the Lord and observe them..." (Numbers 15, 38-39). The large tallit (*tallit gadol*) is made of wool or silk cloth of rectangular shape and at its corners four tassels (*tzitziyot*) are added. At the shorter side of the shawl there are usually also blue or black stripes. The collar of the tallit, *atara*, is often formed by a strip of woven cloth made of gold or silver threads. Jews also use the little tallit (*tallit katan*) worn throughout the day under garments. The little tallit is customarily crocheted or made of linen. There are two kinds of tefillin

– to be worn on the hand and on the head. Each consists of a little black leather box (*bayit*) and straps (*retzuot*) to tie them. The little boxes contain selected passages from biblical texts. When the tefillin are not being used the little boxes are protected by decorated cases. Covering one's head during prayers is a sign of awe and humility which believers feel in God's presence. During synagogue services, as well as during any rites in which the blessing is pronounced, men wear skullcaps or hats. The most frequent head covering is the *kippah* or *yarmulkah*. Women as a rule wear kerchiefs during services.

BEGINNING OF THE SABBATH

The rhythm of daily life is interrupted once a week to celebrate the Sabbath – the day of rest. The purpose is rest and spiritual renewal through prayer and study of the Torah. Linked to the Sabbath is the strict prohibition of all work. The Sabbath is accompanied by many customs included under the term *oneg shabbat* – Sabbath delight. This involves Sabbath meals, festive garments, and sufficient time devoted to sleep. The Sabbath begins on Friday at sunset with the lighting of the Sabbath candles (*nerot shel shabbat*). The ceremony, whether in the synagogue or at home, is carried out before the sun sets when two candles are

7) Pair of Sabbath Candlesticks. Cast, mechanically engraved brass, originally silver-plated, Austria-Hungary, late 19th century

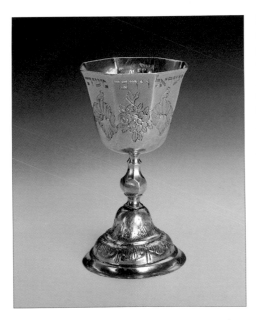

8) Kiddush Cup. Gilt silver, Augsburg, ca. 1760, maker: Franz Christoph Maederl

lit. Lighting the candles, accompanied by a blessing and prayer for the good of the family, is the privilege of women. Following the weekday afternoon prayer comes a special liturgical section known as *Kabbalat Shabbat* (Welcoming the Sabbath), composed primarily of Psalms. The most moving part of the service is the song *Lekhah Dodi*, expressing the idea of a mystical marriage of Israel and Queen Shabbat. After evening prayer the cantor blesses the Sabbath over wine. For this rite, called *Kiddush shel Shabbat* there is a cup (*kos*) usually made of silver or glass. The home feast known as *seudah* starts with a Kiddush and the blessing of two loaves of bread (*barches*, *hallot*). After the food is eaten it is customary to sing songs – *zemirot* – in honour of the Sabbath. The meal ends with a prayer (*Birkat ha-Mazon*). The second Sabbath meal which takes place after the morning Sabbath prayer, is much the same.

9) Seder Zemirot u-Birkat ha-Mazon (Order of the Sabbath Songs and Grace after Meals), Prague, 1514

MORNING AND AFTERNOON
SABBATH SERVICES

The central part of the Sabbath morning synagogue services is the reading from the Torah which takes place after the *Amidah*. This reading is done from a parchment scroll known as *Sefer Torah*. The scroll is wound on two wooden sticks (*atzei hayyim*). The Hebrew text is written in square letters without signs for vowels or a melodic manner of presentation. The scroll can be written only by a professional scri-

10) Torah Mantle. Silk embroidered with metallic threads, Bohemia, 1857. /Donated by Joseph Hayyim ben Wolf Herrmann and his wife Nehama bat Eliezer Hahn/

11) Torah Scroll with Appurtenances: Mantle. Velvet, Prague, 1872. Shield. Silver, late 19th century. Pointer. Silver, Prague, ca. 1890. Crown. Silver, Prague 1866. /The Torah is exhibited in the Ark/

be known as a *sofer*. Religious custom prescribes that the entire Pentateuch be read during the course of a single year. The text is therefore divided into 54 sections – *sedarot* (singular *sidrah*) which are gradually read on the Sabbath. Seven men are called up to the Torah, the first being a *Kohen* (a descendant of Aaron), the second is a *Levite* (a descendant of Levi). Individual portions of the Sidrah are spoken by a reader (*baal koreh*). The eighth to come to the Torah is a *maftir* who chants the portion from the Prophets known as *haftarah*. In terms of content, a haftarah is linked in some way with one of the themes of the Sidrah. Believers pay special respect to the sacred scroll for which they commission various costly appurtenances. One of these in particular is the pointer (*yad*) used to follow the reading of the text. After it is read, the scroll is bound with a Torah binder (*hittul*), clad in a mantle (*meil*) and decorated with a shield (*tas*), a pointer and a pair of finials (*rimmonim*). Sometimes instead of decorating it with finials a metal crown is used – *Keter Torah*. After reading comes the preaching by the rabbi and at the end of the entire morning service is *Musaf* (additional prayer) with a reminder of the Temple offerings. (Musaf is also part of the services for holidays and the New Month). In the afternoon Sabbath prayer part of the next week's Sidrah is read for three persons.

The end of the Sabbath is marked by the third feast of the day *seudah shelishit* which follows afternoon prayer. This meal is accompanied by singing Sabbath songs and the rabbi's sermon. At nightfall comes the evening prayer to which are added biblical passages

12) Havdalah Candles. Wax, early 20th century

13) Spice Box. Hammered and cut-out silver, Central Europe, late 18th century

dealing with the blessing of Israel. The Sabbath ends with a ceremony known as *Havdalah* (separation, distinction) which is the opposite of *Kiddush* (benediction) recited at the beginning of the Sabbath. Havdalah begins by lighting a braided candle with at least four wicks. The flame of Havdalah candles is the first to be lit after Friday evening (it is prohibited to light a fire on the Sabbath). The task of holding the candle, which is sometimes set in a special candlestick, falls to the youngest boy in the family. The cantor (or the father, if Havdalah is said in the home) blesses the wine and then the *besamim* (fragrant spices). The fragrance of spices according to mystical tradition is supposed to soothe a person whose Sabbath soul leaves him. The spice is kept in a decorated, usually silver spice box. The third blessing is said over the flame of the candle. The candle light recalls the first act of creation, God's words "Let there be light!" The man who conducts the ritual takes the goblet and candle and expresses thanks to the Lord for separating the sacred from the mundane, light from darkness, and the seventh day from days of work.

ROSH HA-SHANAH. YOM KIPPUR

The holidays ordained by the Torah are divided into High Holidays and Pilgrim Festivals. Among the High Holidays, also known as Days of Awe or Ten Days of Repentance, are *Rosh ha-Shanah* (New Year) and *Yom Kippur* (Day of Atonement) and the days between them. High Holidays of a serious, solemn character fall on the first autumn month Tishri. The New Year, marked on first and second Tishri, according to tradition is the day of the creation of the world. This holiday, associated with a ban on work, is characterised by its three names: Day of Blowing the Horn, Day of Remembrance, and Day of Judgement. The

14) Torah Pointer Combined with a Spice Box. Cast silver, Bohemia, 1743 (?)

17

first name reflects the biblical commandment to blow a ram's horn (*shofar*); its sound awakens us from moral lassitude and is a reminder of the covenant between the Lord and Israel on Mount Sinai. The second name reflects the need for a person to remember his deeds, while the last name expresses the idea that the whole world is under judgement on this day. God determines who will be inscribed in the book of the dead and who in the book of the living, who is granted wealth and who is condemned to poverty. Through repentance, however, people have a chance to avert an adverse fate. The period of spiritual preparation prior to the holiday reaches its climax in the penitent prayers *Selihot*. In the liturgy of the New Year, apart from the blowing of the horn, the litany *Avinu Malkenu* (Our Father, Our King) is prominent. The story of Isaac's sacrifice, which according to tradition took place on lst Tishri, is read from the Torah. In the af-

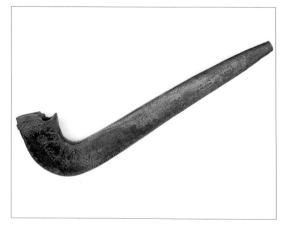

16) Shofar. Engraved horn, Bohemia 1900

18

17) Belt Buckle for the Kittel. Hammered silver, Lvov (Lemberg), 1847, maker: M.K.

ternoon (usually on the first day of the holiday) the ceremony of *tashlikh* is performed on the bank of a river during which believers symbolically throw their sins into the water.

The Days of Repentance culminate on 10th Tishri in the Day of Atonement, the most solemn day in the Jewish calendar. It is not only a day that prohibits labour but it calls for a strict, full day of fasting. The idea of reconciliation with God assumes a previous reconciliation with people. The holiday begins on the eve with the prayer *Kol Nidrei* (All Promises). The daily divine service lasts, with short intervals, until evening. At the end the prayer *Neilah* (Closing the Gates) is read. Among the characteristic elements that belong to the liturgy – besides the litany *Avinu Malkenu* and *Selihot* – is a confession of one's sins (*Vidduy*). The theme of the reading from the Torah and the Musaf prayer is the conciliatory ritual held on Yom Kippur by the High Priest in the Temple of Jerusalem. An important part of the liturgy is the prayer for the dead – *Mazkir*. The prayers for both the High Holy Days and Pilgrim festivals are contained in special prayer books known as *Mahzorim* (singular *Mahzor*).

The most marked outer expression of repentance and surrender to the will of God during the New Year and the Day of Atonement is represented by wearing a shroud (*kittel*). The kittel is a loosely cut garment of white cloth held together with a cloth belt. These belts are sometimes fastened with silver buckles. The white colour expressing humility can be seen during High Holidays as well as on synagogue textiles.

Pesah or Passover together with *Shavuot* and *Succot* belongs to the Pilgrim Festivals. These are the days during which, in Biblical

18) Seder Plate. Engraved pewter, Galicia, mid-18th century

19) Matzah Bag. Velvet embroidered with brightly coloured threads, Moravia 1904

times, men travelled to the Temple of Jerusalem. It brings to mind important events in the history of Israel in connection with harvest celebrations. Passover in the Diaspora is celebrated a total of eight days, from 15th to 22nd Nissan (the holiday usually falls in April). The first two and last two days are holidays that prohibit work, the rest of the days are half-holidays. On Passover, Jews celebrate the liberation of Israel from Egyptian bondage. The name of the holiday is a reminder that during the

20) Seder Dish. China, Vienna, ca. 1900, maker: Josef Vater

Tenth Egyptian plague, God spared, or passed over (Hebrew *pasah*) the houses of Israelites. The holiday is also called *Hag ha-Matzot* (Feast of Unleavened Bread). The most important part of the liturgy is the evening feast known as the *Seder* (order). In the centre of the festive table is a Seder plate, on which are placed three matzot, separated from one another by a textile cover. Five items of food are put on the cover: *zeroah* – a roasted bone recalling the sacrifice of the lamb, *beitzah* – an egg as a reminder of the festive sacrifice, *maror* – bitter herbs as a symbol of the bitterness of slavery, *karpas* – parsley, recalling spring, and *haroset* – a sweet mixture made of fruit, wine and spices, representing the mortar from which Israeli slaves in Egypt made bricks. Sometimes the symbolic food is put directly on the Seder plate, next to which are placed the matzot. During the ceremony the father reads from the Passover Haggadah. The *Haggadah* (story-telling) is a book containing a set of prayers, blessings, stories and songs relating to the Exodus from Egypt. During the festivities four goblets of wine are drunk. On the table a special goblet is prepared for the Prophet Elijah. *Hallel* (a prayer of thanks composed of Psalms) and *Musaf* are recited in the morning synagogue ser-

vice, as during all Pilgrim Festivals. On the Sabbath during the period of half-holidays or on the last day of Passover it is customary to read the scroll of the Song of Songs (*Shir ha-Shirim*).

21) Haggadah shel Pesah (Passover Haggadah). Prague, Katz, 1763

SHAVUOT

22) Mahzor. Prague, Baks, late 17th century. /Liturgical poetry recited on the first day of Shavuot/

The second Pilgrim Festival is *Shavuot* (Feast of Weeks) celebrated in the Diaspora on 6th and 7th Sivan (it usually falls in the second half of May or the first half of June). The name *Shavuot* recalls the seven weeks separating the feast from the start of Passover. This period of 49 days is called *Omer*. The name *omer* was used to designate a sheaf of barley from the new harvest which was brought to the Temple of Jerusalem each day from the second day of Passover until Shavuot.

22

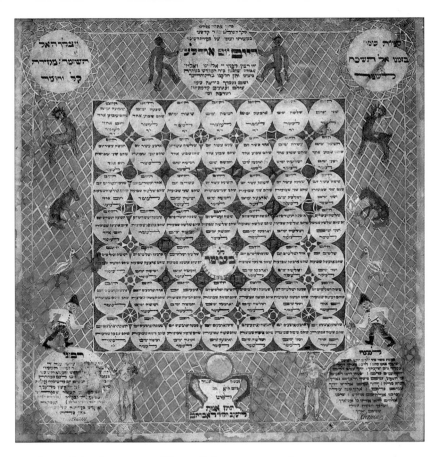

23) Omer Calendar.
Papercut, watercolour,
Bohemia, 1824

The religious commandment to count and proclaim the days of Omer continued even after the Temple was destroyed. The ceremony takes place every day after evening services. An Omer calendar determines the appropriate day. The Hebrew names of the festival in the Torah – *Hag ha-Katzir* – (Festival of the Harvest) and *Hag ha-Bikurim* (Feast of the First Fruits) – point to its agricultural aspect. During the festival pilgrims brought to the Temple the first fruits of the new wheat harvest. But in the celebration of Shavuot its historical-spiritual level is emphasised above all. The Feast of Weeks is the anniversary of the day when the Lord declared the Ten Commandments (*Aseret ha-*

24) Omer Calendar. Wood, parchment, Bohemia, ca. 1800

-*Dibrot*) and presented Moses with the Torah. Acceptance of this brings to a spiritual climax the liberation of Israel from physical slavery. The biblical Book of Ruth forms an important part of the divine service.

SUCCOT, SHEMINI ATZERET, SIMHAT TORAH

At the end of September or in October, not quite a week after the Day of Atonement, the last of the Pilgrim Festivals begins. *Succot* (Feast of the Tabernacles) is celebrated seven days, from 15th to 21st Tishri. The following day is *Shemini Atzeret* (Eighth Day of Solemn Assembly). The ninth day (23rd Tishri) known as *Simhat Torah* (Rejoicing of the Law) is also

25) Ethrog Container. Chased and gilt silver, Augsburg, ca. 1675, maker: EB

celebrated in the Diaspora. Work is prohibited on the first and last two days of the nine--day period. The other days are half-holidays. *Succot* is characterised by the commandment to spend seven days in tabernacles or booths. The tabernacle (*sukkah*) is a provisional structure covered with twigs of deciduous trees or conifer branches. A stay in the sukkah is a reminder that before settling in the Promised Land the Israelites had to wander in the desert for forty years. Succot was also a celebration of the vineyard harvest and garden crops. Thanking God for everything that the Earth has given man is expressed by the ceremony of waving the bouquet of *lulav*. The latter consists of *etrog* (the fruit of the citron, related to that of the lemon tree), *lulav* (a branch of the date palm), *hadasim* (three little branches of myrtle) and *aravot*

26) Siddur. Manuscript on parchment, Central Europe, 15th century. /Ceremony of Hoshanot/

(two willow branches). A bouquet of twigs held together with *etrog* is waved during the laudatory prayer *Hallel* and the ceremony of *Hoshanot* – a procession around a scroll of the Torah placed on the platform. In the prayers during Hoshanot entreaties are repeated for salvation and renewal of the Temple. The seventh day of the holidays, when a total of seven solemn circles are walked around the Torah, is called *Hoshanah Rabbah*. Etrog is usually kept in a special little box or bowl. On the Sabbath during the half-holidays it is customary to read the Book of Ecclesiastes (*Kohelet*). A prominent part of the *Shemini Atzeret* is the *Musaf* with prayers for rain. The year-round reading from the Torah comes to an end during *Simhat Torah* which also marks the beginning of a new reading. The celebrations are accompanied by processions with all the scrolls of the Torah that are housed in the synagogue.

DAYS OF SORROW

27) Kinot le-Tisha be-Av (Dirges for the 9th Av). Brno, F.J. Neumann 1760

Tisha be-Av (Fast of the 9th Av) is of greatest importance among the days of sorrow. This day, which generally falls at the end of July or beginning of August, recalls several tragic events in Jewish history, chiefly the destruction of the first and second Temples of Jerusalem (586 B.C.E. and 70 C.E.). The 9th Av is a day of strict fasting and lasts from sunset to sunset. The temple curtain in synagogues is taken down and the Holy Ark is covered with black cloth. During divine services worshippers sit on low stools or on the floor, as a sign of mourning. In the

מקום מקדשינו

כותל מערבי

28) Tefillin Bag. Jerusalem (?), late 19th century

evening services the *Ekha* (Lamentations of Jeremiah) and the dirges (*Kinot*) are read out. The *Kinot* are read also during morning services when, as a sign of sorrow, neither the tallit nor tefillin are worn. Other days of sorrow include the Fast of the 10th Tevet (*Asarah be-Tevet*) which commemorates the beginning of the siege of Jerusalem by Nebuchadnezzar in 587 B.C.E. and the Fast of the 15th Tammuz (*Shivah Asar be-Tammuz*), recalling the subsequent breach of Jerusalem's walls. Another day when no food is eaten is the Fast of Gedalia (*Tzom Gedalya*) in memory of the murder of Jewish governor of Judea, which occurred on 3rd Tishri. In the liturgy of the days of fasting these tragic events are remembered in the penitent prayers *Selihot*.

HANUKKAH

Hanukkah (Feast of Dedication) is celebrated for eight days from 25th Kislev to 2nd Tevet (usually in December). This holiday recalls the victory of the Jews over the army of Antiochus IV, the Seleucid ruler of Syria who, under the threat of death, prohibited Jews from performing circumcision and other biblical commandments and who desecrated the Temple by introducing idolatry. After three years of struggle, the uprising led by Priest Mattathias and his sons led to the liberation of Jerusalem and the purification and rededication of the Temple. An important role in this was played by the lighting of the seven-branched candelabrum (*menorah*). After the enemy fled, only one dish of undefiled oil was found in the Temple which was enough to last only a single day. But a miracle occurred and the oil continued to burn in the menorah for eight whole days before new oil was prepared. In honour of this event lights are kindled at home for eight days in an eight-branched candelabrum called *Hanukkiyah*. One light is lit the first evening, and throughout the course of the holiday one more light is lit each evening. A special light, the *shames* (servant), is used to light the candles. Lighting the candelabrum is accompanied by

29) Hanukkah Lamp. Cast brass, Bohemia, first half of the 19th century. / 'Menorah' type/

30) Hanukkah Lamp. Cast brass, Bohemia, early 19th century. /'Bench' type/

31) Torah Curtain. Velvet embroidered with metallic threads, Moravia (Jemnice?), 1812. /Donated by Simon ben Leib Jemnitz and his wife Hindl/

a blessing and the hymn *Maoz Tzur Yeshuati* (The Rocky Fort of my Salvation). Hanukkiyot are of diverse shape. Originally the most common type of Hanukkiyah was shaped like a bench with eight oil burners. From the 19th century the prevailing type of Hanukkiyah resembled Temple candelabrum. This "menorah" has eight branches (the ninth branch is not in line with the others and is intended for the *shames*). In the last two centuries the little oil lamps in the Hanukkiyot were replaced by candles. In synagogue liturgy the Hallel is read on Hanukkah days. Among household customs that accompany this holiday mention should be made of the children's game called top *(dreidel).*

32) Torah Shield. Chased silver, partially gilt, Prague, 1708, maker: Jan Kogler

PURIM

Purim (Feast of Lots) falls on 14th Adar and in a leap year on 14th Vaadar. In both instances it comes one month before Passover, i.e., usually in March. Purim is the most joyous

33) Esther Approaching King Ahasuerus. Embroidery on paper, wool, beads, Bohemia, mid-19th century

34) Megillat Ester (Scroll of Esther). Manuscript on parchment, pen-and-ink drawings in sepia, 18th century

of all the Jewish holidays recalling events that took place in the Persian Empire during the reign of King Ahasuerus (4th century B.C.E.). The perfidious Vizier Haman tried to wipe out all the Jews in the empire; lots were cast for the most suitable date of this plan. (The name of the holiday comes from the Persian word for a lot – *pur*.) Thanks to the courage of Queen Esther and her uncle Mordechai, however, this plan was foiled. In memory of these events it is one's duty to keep the Fast of Esther (*Taanit Ester*) on 13th Adar, one day before the holiday. The main section of the Purim observance is the reading of the Esther scroll (*Megillat Ester*). The *Megillah* is read out at evening and morning services. The scroll, read by the cantor is written on parchment in square letters. The *Megillot*, from which those attending divine services follow the reading, are usually richly illustrated. During the reading, whenever Haman's name is mentioned, it is drowned by the noise of rattles. Purim is usually celebrated with lively banquets. Particularly popular are the masquerade processions and theatre performances about Queen Esther. Religious duties involve giving gifts to the poor and sending presents to friends. This custom is known as *mishloah manot* (*Schlachmones*), which literally means "the sending of portions".

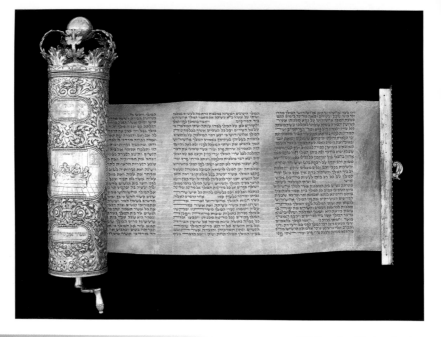

YOM HA-SHOAH, YOM HA-ZIK-KARON, YOM HA-ATZMAUT

35) Scroll of Esther in the Case. Manuscript on parchment, silver, partially gilt, Vienna, ca. 1880. /Depiction of the royal banquet/

The festivals that have been most recently included in the religious year commemorate both the most tragic and the most joyful events of modern Jewish history. The death of six million Jews is recalled on the Day of Remembrance for the Victims of the Holocaust, known in Hebrew as *Yom ha-Shoah*. In Israel this is commemorated on 27th Nisan and in the Diaspora on 19 April, which is the anniversary of the Warsaw Ghetto uprising of 1943. The service on *Yom ha-Shoah* contains a special prayer for Jewish martyrs. Commemorative ceremonies for those who perished defending the State of Israel take place on *Yom ha-Zikkaron*, the Day of Remembrance for those who Fell in Battle, which is on 4th Iyyar. The joyful holiday, Israel's Independence Day, is celebrated the following day on 5th Iyyar. (The Jewish State gained independence on 5th Iyyar 5708 –

14 May 1948). *Yom ha-Atzmaut* is connected with various civil and religious celebrations. The divine service includes the haftarah from the Prophet Isaiah foretelling the coming of the Messiah.

Synagogue is a word of Greek origin meaning *assembly*. The name corresponds to the meaning of the Hebrew term for synagogue *bet kneset* (house of assembly). The synagogue is used chiefly for services but it is also a place for study and a social centre. The most important position in this institution is held by the rabbi (*rav*), the spiritual leader of the community and an expert in religious law. His role in the services is that of a preacher. Any adult male, in fact, can lead a divine service but as a rule the recitation of prayers is performed by the cantor (*hazzan*) who apart from having an excellent knowledge of prayers and Hebrew, must also have a pleasant voice. The elected representative responsible for the conduct of the service and administering financial matters is the *gabbai* (treasurer). The assistant of the gabbai is the *shamash*, "*shames*" (servant).

36) Lions of the Ark at Bechyně. Painted wood, Bohemia, ca. 1820

The most important object in the synagogue is the Holy Ark (*aron ha-kodesh*) in which the Torah scrolls are kept. This stands at the eastern wall or is built into it. The door of the Holy Ark which is usually decorated with tablets of the Decalogue and figural lions, is covered by

the synagogue curtain (*parokhet*). A valance, known as a *kaporet*, is suspended above it. Hanging in front of the Holy Ark is the eternal light (*ner tamid*). A raised pulpit known as a *bimah* or an *almemor* is used for reading the Torah and preaching. The bimah, usually surrounded

37) V.Kandler, Interior of the Old-New Synagogue. Engraving, ca. 1835

34

by a decorative grille, is in the centre of the hall in traditional synagogues (from the 19th century it was often moved to a raised podium in front of the Holy Ark). During the reading the Torah is laid on the table (*shulhan*). An important part of the synagogue equipment is the pulpit known as *ammud* (column) situated to the right, in front of the Holy Ark. The cantor leads the service from this pulpit. The place where the *hazzan* stands as a sign of humility is located below the floor level. At the head of the pulpit there usually is a tablet with a Hebrew verse *Shiviti ha-Shem le-negdi tamid*

38) Lavabo. Hammered copper and brass, Olomouc, ca. 1880

39) Alms Box. Wood, hammered brass, Bohemia (Sušice?) 1790

(I have set the Lord always before me). Many other items are part of the synagogue interior such as the candlesticks, the lavabo, tablets with texts of benediction, and alms boxes. The seats were originally positioned along the walls of the hall. If the bimah was moved to the Holy Ark, the seats were laid out in straight rows facing East. During traditional divine services men and women remain separated. In synagogues one therefore finds a special place reserved for women for which the term *weiberschul* (women's school) or *ezrat nashim* (women's courtyard) is used. For the most part the women's prayer room is on the balcony, but it can be in a separate room joined to the main aisle by windows. If women and men are in the same hall, they are separated by a curtain (*mehitza*).

SYNAGOGUE AND TEMPLE

41) Valance. Velvet embroidered with metallic threads, Moravia 1748

The Temple of Jerusalem was the heart of Israel. After the destruction of the Temple the focus of religious life shifted to synagogues. Faith in the rebuilding of the Temple have, however, never waned. The synagogue stresses the bond to its spiritual model by, for example, using the names of the Temple appurtenances to indicate parts of the synagogue equipment. The most sacred object in the Holy of Holies was the Ark (chest) of Testimony (*aron ha-kodesh*) with the tablets of the Ten Commandments. The cover of the chest, known as the "mercy seat" (Heb. *kapporet*), was adorned with two gold statues of cherubs. The Holy of Holies was separated from the Holy Place by a curtain known as a *parokhet*. A seven-branched candelabrum – a *menorah* – with its eternal light (*ner tamid*) made certain that the Temple was never in darkness. All these objects find their parallel in the synagogue. The Ark of Testimony with the Decalogue has its counter-

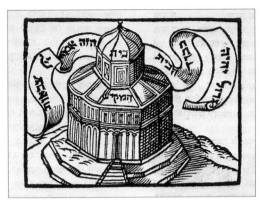

part in the Holy Ark with the Torah scrolls. The Temple curtain corresponds in function and name (*parokhet*) to the synagogue curtain. The name *kapporet* was used to denote the valance hanging over the curtain. The function of the menorah is fulfilled by the eternal light. One comes across the terminology and symbolism associated with the Temple and its ritual even in the appurtenances of the Torah scroll. The Torah mantle and shield are connected with the mantle and breast-shield of the High Priest. The wooden rollers on which the Torah scroll is rolled, are regarded as the symbolic imitation of two powerful Temple columns known as *Boaz* and *Yakhin*. The finials on the rollers – *rimmonim*

40) Moses Isserles, Sefer Torat ha-Ola (Teachings of the Burnt Offering), Prague, Mordechai ben Gershon Katz 1569. /Vignette depicting the Temple/

(pomegranates) – are comparable to the capitals of the Temple columns (in decorating the capitals the motif of the pomegranate was used). Boaz and Yakhin also appear in the decoration of the synagogue curtains and shields.

42) Curtain. Velvet, appliqué, Prague 1658. /Donated by Eliezer, son of Moses Bendiner, and his wife Hayya to the Old-New Synagogue/

43) Torah Shield. Hammered and chased silver, Moravia (?), second half of the 18th century

The Temple furnishings are most often depicted on the valance – here one can seen the seven-branched candelabrum, the altar for whole-offerings, the altar for burning incense, the table for show-bread and the basin for ablution used by the priest. Parts of the clothing of the High Priest often appear on the valances – especially the headband and the breast-shield which was set in a special garment called *efod*.

KLAUSEN SYNAGOGUE

The Klausen Synagogue acquired its name after three smaller buildings known as *klausen* (from the Latin *claustrum*) which the Jewish mayor Mordechai Maisel built here in the late 16th century and which were destroyed by fire on 21 June 1689. The *klausen* were used as a ritual bath, a Talmudic school (where Rabbi Löw taught) and a synagogue. A new Baroque building was built on the site in 1694. The Ark, completed in 1696, was built at the expense of the Viennese banker Samuel Oppenheim. There was a partial reconstruction of the synagogue in 1883-1884 which included an extension of the western part of the building and an adjustment of the women's gallery. At the same time the bimah, originally located in the middle of the hall, was moved in front of the tabernacle. The reconstruction, carried out according to a design by Bedřich Münzberger, basically retained the Baroque character of the building and it was left undisturbed even by a complex restoration carried out from 1979 to 1984. The last reconstruction of the synagogue between 1995 and 1996 exposed the bimah foundations and the pavement of the original synagogue from 1694.

44) Synagogue Clock. Bohemia 1884. /Donated by Sigmund Reach to the Klausen Synagogue/

Gallery of the Klausen Synagogue

45) Torah Mantle. Velvet embroidered with metallic threads, Prague 1696. /Donated by Joel Petschi to the Klausen Synagogue/

THE COURSE
OF LIFE

The most important moments in an individual's life – birth, reaching adulthood, wedding, illness and death – are not simply biological processes and statistical facts, for they all have a spiritual dimension. In Judaism, which represents a specific way of life, they offer an opportunity to carry out the religious commandments (*mitzvot*).

BIRTH

Birth represents a time when the lives of the mother and child are in greatest danger. Both their family and the whole community pray for their health. During the Sabbath service, the father is called up to the Torah, and af-

46) Amulet for a Newborn Boy. Woodcut, Germany (Sulzbach?), 18th century. /A depiction of a circumcision (above) and of Adam and Eve (at the sides). From the Genizah in Luže/

קודש לה׳
זן לכבוד המקום ולכוד
התורה כה׳ יעקב אויער
עזי מֿ יטֿל תי מוֿלֿךֿ
פילזֿען ,עֿבֿוֿר בֿנֿיֿהֿם
הֿיֿלֿד מֿטֿה שֿי׳ וֿאֿחֿיֿו
הֿיֿלֿד שֿמֿוֿאֿל שֿי׳ הֿוֿבֿא
אֿלֿ הֿקֿוֿדֿש

47) Torah Mantle. Embroidered silk, Plzeň, 1866. /Donated by Jacob Auer on the birth of his sons Moses and Samuel/

ter the reading there is a formal public blessing (*mi she-berakh le-yoledet*) with wishes of health for mother and child. Girls are given their names at this blessing. A period of purification for the mother begins a week after the birth of a boy or two weeks after the birth of a girl and lasts 33 or 66 days respectively. When this period ends, the mother goes to the ritual bath (*mikveh*) and then visits the synagogue. In traditional society, fear for the lives of mothers and children led to the use of protective amulets (*kameot*). Belief in their effectiveness was influenced by various currents of Kabbalistic thought. Amulets principally contain Hebrew biblical quotations. Above the mother's bed or the door usually hung a paper board or a cut-out known as a *kimpet-zetl* (the Yiddish word *kimpet* is derived from the German *Kindbett*, i.e., childbed or isolation). Above all, amulets were supposed to protect from *Lilith* – according to legend the spurned first wife of Adam who threatens all new-born children. Most amulets protecting the mother and new-born child contain Psalm 121 and the names of protective angels. With the spread of Jewish Enlightenment, however, the use of amulets as a protection against Lilith was abandoned during the 19th century.

CIRCUMCISION

It is through the covenant of circumcision (Heb. *brit mila*) that the boy enters into a sacred relationship with God and with his community. "And you shall circumcise the flesh of your foreskin; and it shall be the sign of the covenant between me and you. And every male among you shall be circumcised at the age of eight days", (Genesis 17, 11-12). Circumcision expresses the idea of subjecting the body to a moral law, the ignoring of which was and still is an outward sign of forsaking the faith. The circumci-

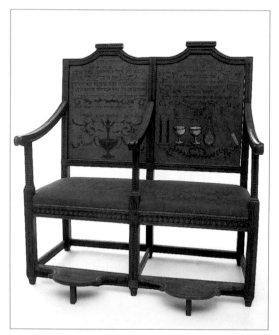

48) Circumcision Chair. Wood, damask, Údlice, ca. 1805. /On the back are circumcision blessings and depictions of the circumcision implements/

49) Cradle. Wood, Moravia, early 19th century

50) Circumcision Implements. Silver, steel, glass, latter half of the 19th century

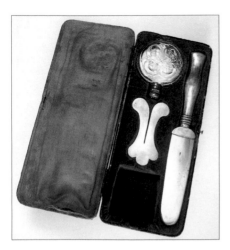

sion is carried out either in the home or in the synagogue. According to rabbinic tradition, an invisible guest – the prophet Elijah – is present at every circumcision as witness and protector of the boy. A special cup (*kos shel Eliyahu*) is prepared for Elijah. The circumcision chair is also named after the prophet – *kise shel Eliyahu*. In this country the Elijah chair usually has two parts, a symbolic seat reserved for Elijah and a seat for the *sandak* (godfather) whose task is to hold the boy on his lap during the operation.

The actual circumcision – the removal of the foreskin – is carried out by the *mohel*, a pious man with the required medical and ritual knowledge. For the operation he uses a special knife with two blades and a round point. These days the wound is treated with modern medicaments but in the past, use was made of traditional healing ointments and powder which were kept in richly ornamented vials and boxes. The circumcision ceremony is blessed by the *mohel*, the father and all those present. An important part of the liturgy is the *mohel's* prayer in which the boy is given his Hebrew name. In the Ashkenazi region a custom has survived whereby the boy is named after a late relative. Rules concerning the circumcision and relevant liturgical texts were recorded in special handbooks known as *Mohelbuchs*. These were usually richly illustrated manuscripts, particularly renowned examples of which are those created by the 18th century artist-scribes of the Moravian school of penmanship. The *mohel* kept a book of the circumcised (*sefer nimmolim*) which was similar to a registry of births.

51) Dinei ve-Tefillot ha-Shayakhim le-Brit Milah (Circumcision Rules and Prayers). Manuscript on parchment, tempera, Vienna, 1727/8, scribe: Aaron ben Benjamin Zeev of Jevíčko (Gewitsch)

52) Circumcision screen. Oil on canavas, Bohemia (?), 1764. /Donated by Isaac ben Abraham and his wife Hanele bat Tzvi on the birth of their son Abraham. In the centre are circumcision blessings, around are biblical scenes/

In Bohemia and Moravia, as in other Ashkenazi regions, it is customary to present the synagogue with a Torah binder in honour of the birth of a son. The binder (known in Hebrew as *hittul* or *mappah*, and in German as *Wimpel*) is a long and narrow strip of cloth which is used to bind the Torah scroll after readings. The *hittul* is sewn of three or four strips made from the cloth in which the boy was wrapped during circumcision. Torah binders are usually made of linen and decorated with embroidery. The Hebrew inscription includes the names of the boy and parents as well as the blessing which ends the circumcision ceremony: "May God raise him to the Torah, the marriage canopy, and good deeds!" The most common decoration on binders includes embroidery depicting a rolled up Torah scroll and a wedding canopy. On some binders there are signs of the zodiac under which the boy was

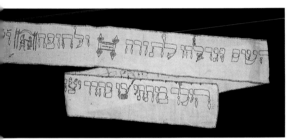

53) Torah Binder. Embroidered linen, Bohemia, 1778. /Donated on the birth of Matityahu ben Isaac/

54) Torah Binder. Embroidered linen, Moravia, 1737. /Donated on the birth of Elazar ben Elazar. The posthumous child was born under the sign of Virgo/

born. Only rarely does the following text appear on the binder: "Be brave as a leopard, light as an eagle, swift as a deer and strong as a lion!" (Avot 5, 20), in which case the text is accompanied by a depiction of the above animals.

REDEMPTION OF THE FIRST-BORN

A fundamental religious duty connected with birth is the Redemption of the First-Born (*pidyon ha-ben*). Redemption concerns boys who are born as the first child of a mother (but not those whose father or mother are Levites or Kohens). The first-born of Israel were dedicated to the service of God and performed the duties of priests. After they took part in the worship of the golden calf, they lost their status in the divine service and were replaced by men from the Levi tribe. In memory of the original dedication the first-born (*bekhor*) is redeemed. The ceremony is held on the thirty-first day following birth.

55) Tray for the Pidyon ha-Ben Ceremony. Chased silver, Austria-Hungary, late 19th century, maker: FV

The father presents the boy to the *Kohen*, the descendant of the High Priest Aaron, and after answering his questions declares that he wishes to redeem his son and pay five silver shekel for him. The *kohen* then announces the redemption and gives the boy a priestly blessing. Various silver coins are used for the redemption, but together they must contain at least 101 grams of pure silver. It is customary for the coins to be handed over on silver plates or trays which are often decorated with a depiction of the Binding of Isaac.

One of the fundamental duties of a father is to ensure that his children are brought up in the spirit of Judaism. He alone usually guides the child through the first steps of religious practice and later secures his or her participation in various forms of religious education. Traditionally only boys were sent to school, while girls were educated in the home. Boys went to the Jewish elementary school (*heder*) at an early age, usually at 5, and then moved up to the upper level school (*yeshivah*). Both types of schools were focused almost exclusively on religious subjects. From the beginning of the Enlightenment, Jewish schools emerged which placed greater emphasis on general educational subjects. Following the gradual decline of independent Jewish education in the late 19th century, religious education was transferred to religious lessons at non-denominational state schools.

The attainment of adulthood is an important moment in life. A Jewish boy is considered an adult at the age of thirteen years, a girl at twelve. A boy becomes a *bar mitzvah* (son of commandment), a girl a *bat mitzvah* (daughter of commandment). This means that from then on they assume full res-

56) Robert Guttmann, Bar Mitzvah. Oil on canvas, 1941

57) Isidor Kaufmann, Portrait of a Boy. Oil on wood, ca. 1880

ponsibility for their behaviour in the religious sphere. The boy is proclaimed a *bar mitzvah* at a ceremony which is held in the synagogue on the first Sabbath after his thirteenth birthday. He is solemnly called to the Torah and is usually honoured with reciting the weekly section from the Prophets – *haftarah*. It is on this occasion that he wears the large prayer shawl (*tallit gadol*) for the first time. The service is followed by a festive meal at which he usually gives a short sermon (*pshetl*). One of the signs of the acceptance of all religious pledges is the right and duty to wear *tefillin* (phylacteries) during morning prayers on weekdays. The *bat mitzvah* ceremony does not have a fixed form. Girls usually give a talk on a theme from the Torah in the synagogue or community hall.

58) Tefillin Bag. Embroidered velvet, appliqué, Bohemia, first half of the 19th century

Boys usually receive gifts which are directly connected with their new rights and duties – principally the large prayer shawl and phylacteries, along with decorative bags. While the *tallit* and *tefillin* have always been made by a specially trained expert, the *sofer* (scribe), the making of various bags used to be the work of the female relatives of the boy. *Tefillin* bags are mostly made of velvet, although some are crocheted and macramé. Towards the end of the 19th century, factory-made silk bags emerged alongside the domestically made products. Other popular gifts include skull-caps (*kippot*). Among the more expensive gifts are Sabbath candlesticks, and books in rich bindings.

59) Meir ben Samuel Edeles, Zikhron Ahava u-Teshuvat Nedavah, helek bet (Reminder of Love and Voluntary Repentance, Second Part). Manuscript on paper, Bohemia, 1833. /Donated by the author to his son Mordechai on the occasion of his bar mitzvah. The book contains explanations of the Bible and original poetry/

Women and marriage are held in great respect in Judaism and are lauded in many passages of the Bible. Marriage is based on mutual trust and agreement, which is expressed by the drawing up of a marriage contract (*ketubbah*) prior to the wedding. The *ketubbah*, written in Aramaic, stipulates the rights and mutual pledges of husband and wife. Above all, it contains the husband's commitment to respect his wife and never to leave her in want. The *ketubbah* also secures the material provision for the wife in the event of the husband's death or divorce. The drawing up of the *ketubbah*, which is often richly ornamented, is usually the responsibility of the scribe. The wedding ceremony takes place below the *huppah* (wedding canopy) which symbolises the future home of the couple. This is held on four poles and is erected either in the open air or in the synagogue. The first to enter the *huppah* is the bridegroom (*hatan*) who is accompanied by his parents, best men and witnesses. Then comes the bride (*kallah*) along with her parents and bridesmaids. She makes seven circuits around the bridegroom, which marks the beginning of the first part of the ceremony, the be-

60) Ketubah. Tempera and ink on parchment, Ferarra, 1715. /Wedding contract between Samuel ben Solomon Moses Cavallieri and Sarah bat Moses Simon Basilea of Verona, 1. Adar sheni 5475/

61) Wedding Wreath and Veil. Waxed cloth, tulle, leaves, gilt wood frame, 19th century

62) Wedding Ring. Engraved silver, Bohemia (?), 19th century

trothal (*erussin*). This is when the Rabbi or the *hazzan* gives the betrothed the first wine in wedlock. The engagement becomes legally valid after the bridegroom places a ring on the forefinger of the bride and pronounces the ancient formula: "With this ring you are consecrated to me according to the law of Moses and Israel." The ring (*tabaat*) may not be adorned with jewels. In some communities it was customary to lend the betrothed a special ring for the ceremony which was adorned with a miniature house. The betrothal is followed by the reading of the *ketubbah* which leads to the second part of the ceremony – the marriage (*nissuin*). During the *nissuin*, the *hazzan* sings seven benedictions and the couple drink a second cup of wine together. At the end of the ceremony the bridegroom breaks a glass after which all present call out "*Mazal tov!*"

(Good luck!) With the shattering of the glass, the Rabbis' admonishment is carried out that people, even in the happiest moments of life, should not forget the destruction of the Temple. The bride wears a fashionable period dress which is usually white. A specific feature is the wearing of a veil to cover the face. In so doing, the bride follows Rebecca, who took a veil when Isaac, her husband-to-be, came to meet her. Wedding veils, especially in towns, used to be transparent and made of silk with metallic fringes. In rural areas the bride would wear a head covering which consisted of an oblong piece of usually silk material that was wrapped around and tied with ribbons.

WEDDING FEAST AND GIFTS

The ceremony is followed by a wedding feast, often with dancing. Traditionally, music was provided by a Jewish *Klezmer* group and

63) Plate. Engraved pewter, Pilsen, after 1802, maker: Josef Kuntzel. /Doron derasha for the bridegroom Kopel Langsfeld of Golčův Jeníkov, donated in 1830/

guests were entertained by a jester (*badkhen*). It was customary during the feast for the bridegroom to give a sermon (*derasha*) on various themes from the Bible and the Talmud. In return he would be presented with a gift (*doron derasha*) which was prepared for the occasion. In this country these gifts mostly consisted of engraved pewter plates which were usually commissioned by pious associations. Other gifts presented to the bridegroom during the meal included religious literature and liturgical objects. Brides received Sabbath candlesticks, jewels and prayer-books in rich binding, in addition to various practical items for the home, such as tablecloths, covers and Sabbath textiles. The bride's presents were often presented a week before the wedding.

DIVORCE AND HALITZAH

Jewish religion admits divorce (*gerushin*), but the rabbinic court grants permission only in exceptional cases. The husband must then give his wife a bill of divorce (*get*). This has a precisely set form and content and, amongst other things, must contain the names of both parties and of two witnesses, the date and place of the dissolution of marriage. As a rule, a *get* is written down by a *sofer*. Jewish marriage law knows Levirate marriage, called *yibbum* in Hebrew. According to the Torah, if the husband dies after a childless marriage, it is the duty of his brother to marry the widow. The first-born son of this union bears the name of the deceased. If the brother rejects such a marriage, he has to undergo a ceremony known as *halitzah* (taking off the shoes), during which his brother's widow removes his right shoe in front of witnesses. This act frees both of the mutual obligation. A special leather shoe with three loops and a strap is used for the ceremony.

THE JEWISH HOME

As to its outside appearance a Jewish home does not greatly differ from others in its neighbourhood. What is unique, however, is a case that is attached to all door posts – the *mezuzah*. A typical interior feature of the home is a wall plaque (*mizrah*) which indicates the direction of prayers. In the past, living conditions for the urban Jewish population were affected by the overcrowding of the ghettos – it was not uncommon for a single room to be shared by two families. The situation was somewhat bet-

64) Interior of a Rustic Kitchen

65) Interior of a Parlour

ter in the smaller towns and villages. After leaving the ghettos in the latter half of the nineteenth century, the majority of Jews in this country enjoyed a middle class standard of living. There are only a few visible differences in the furnishings and utensils used by Jewish and Christian families.

MEZUZAH AND MIZRAH

The *mezuzah* is a parchment scroll placed inside an oblong case that is affixed to the upper right-hand door post of the entry to the house and each of its living rooms. It is attached in a sloping position with the top pointing

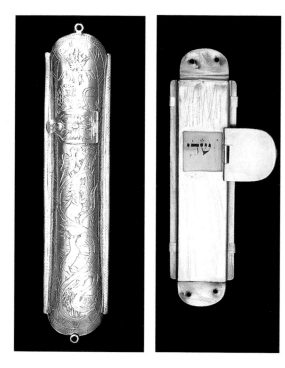

66–68) Mezuzot.
/Engraved silver, early
19th century
/Brass, late 19th century
/Carved wood, early 20th
century

inward. On the scroll are inscribed two biblical passages which form part of the *Shema Yisrael* prayer(Deuteronomy 6, 4-9; 11, 13-21). The mezuzah is a sign recalling the presence of God and a commitment to his commandments – "Hear, O Israel! the Lord is our God, the Lord is One. You shall love the Lord your God with all your heart, with all your soul, and with all your might. And these words which I command you this day shall be in your heart. You shall teach them diligently to your children and you shall inscribe them on the door posts of your house and on your gates." Mezuzah cases are usually fashioned from metal, wood, leather and now plastic.

Mizrah (Heb. East) is a plaque which is hung on the eastern wall of the house to indicate the direction of prayers. As far as the text is concerned, the simplest types only bear the word

Mizrah, while the more intricate contain various biblical quotations, e.g., Psalm 121. The majority of *mizrahim* which used to be made in the home were coloured papercuts. Velvet and silk *mizrahim* decorated with embroidery and appliqué were also made in the home. Painted glass *mizrahim* that were made by local folk artists could also be found in village households. It was also customary to use purchased *mizrahim* that were made with the help of various graphic techniques.

69) Mizrah. Hand-painted papercut, Vonoklasy, 1816, maker: Ezekiel Popper

KASHRUT. RITUAL SLAUGHTER

Characteristic of the Jewish household is the observance of the rules governing the ritual purity of food – *kashrut* (derived from *kasher*, i.e., ritually clean). Above all, Jewish law states which animals may be consumed and which for reasons of impurity may not. Ritually clean mammals are those that chew the cud and have split hooves, i.e., cattle, sheep, goats and deer. Pork is strictly prohibited, as are all beasts of prey and rodents etc. Among the birds that may be eaten are the domesticated varieties, i.e., hens, geese, ducks, turkeys and pigeons, in addition to pheasants, partridges and quails. Prohibited are birds of prey and owls, as well as storks and herons etc. Only those fish that have fins and scales may be consumed. Prohibited are all kinds of reptiles, amphibians, crustaceans and molluscs. For meat to be ritually clean a special method of slaughter (*shehitah*)

must be adhered to. This applies to mammals and birds but not to fish. Ritual slaughter may only be carried out by a specially trained expert, the *shohet*, who uses a special knife to cut the animal's throat. The manner of slaughter is cho-

71) Koshering Board, Knife and Choppers. Wood, steel, late 19th and early 20th century

sen to ensure that the animal does not suffer and that the blood drains out of the body. The consumption of blood is strictly prohibited. Any blood that remains is removed during "koshering", when the meat is soaked in cold water for at least half an hour and after draining is covered with salt. The meat is then left on a koshering board for excess blood to drain away and is washed an hour later. Another basic principle of *kashrut* is the consistent separation of meat and dairy produce. Any mixture of meat and milk is strictly forbidden; separate sets of utensils must be used for preparing and serving meat and milk dishes.

PESAH CUISINE

The eating of *hametz* is prohibited during the eight-day spring festival of Pesah. Hametz means food prepared from leavened flour of wheat, rye, barley, oats or spelt. The prohibition applies to bread as well as to beverages made from fermented grain, such as beer. For Jews in the Ashkenazi regions hametz includes even rice and pulses. Yeast (*seor*) is naturally prohibited. Hametz and seor may not even be kept in the house, which means they have to be removed before the start of the holiday. Pesah is therefore preceded by a thorough cleaning of the whole house. To prevent Pesah food coming into contact with even the tiniest remnants of hametz it is customary to use a special set of dishes exclusively for this festival. Unleavened

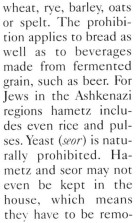

72) Matzah Rollers. Wood, iron, 19th century

61

bread (*matzah*) and food using matzah flour is eaten during the Pesah. Matzah is prepared from pure flour and water and is baked immediately after kneading so as to prevent any possibility of fermentation. The surface can be pierced by large wooden rollers with metal spikes or special combs. In the past, matzah flour was prepared at home by grating baked matzahs with special iron graters.

CEREMONIAL OBJECTS IN THE HOME

Every Jewish home contains various ceremonial objects which are primarily connected with the Sabbath. Sabbath candlesticks for the Sabbath lights, *kiddush* cups, *hallah* (bread) covers and Sabbath plates are all used to celebrate the beginning of the Sabbath. Cups, covers and plates are also used during the Sabbath meal. To mark the close of the Sabbath, use is made of Havdalah objects – holders or candlesticks with braided Havdalah candles, spice boxes and various plates and trays. Hanukkah menorahs, ethrog containers and Pesah plates can also be found in the home. The material and design of ritual objects for the home naturally depend on the financial position and the particular taste of each family. Havdalah spice boxes have always attracted the interest of collectors.

Ceremonial Hall of the Burial Society

73) Torah Mantle. Velvet embroidered with metallic and silk threads, Prague, 1862. /Donated by Serel Pascheles in commemoration of her late husband Wolf/

ILLNESS AND DEATH
IN JUDAISM

People must not be left alone at times of illness and death. Visiting the sick (*bikkur holim*) and attending the funeral (*halvayat ha-met*) are fundamental religious requirements. Whilst it is the task of every Jew to fulfil these duties, the main responsibility for paying regular visits to the terminally ill and for arranging a proper burial is assumed by a group of volunteers – the burial society – usually known as the *hevrah kaddisha de-gomle hassadim* (the holy society of those who perform acts of mercy). The members of this society provide the sick and their close relatives both with practical assistance and spiritual comfort. The order of prayers for the sick, the dying and the deceased, during the ritual washing and dressing of the body and during the burial is defined in the book *Maavar Yabbok* (Crossing the Yabbok) as written down by the

74) Aaron Berekhya mi-Modena, Maavar Yabbok (Crossing the Jabbok). Manuscript on parchment, tempera, Mikulov (Nikolsburg), 1721/2, scribe: Samuel Hayyim ben Yuda Finkls of the Reik family

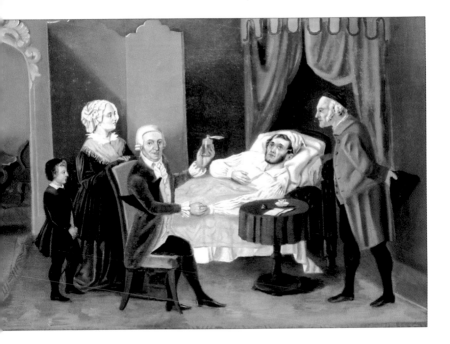

75) Anonymous Artist, Visiting the Sick Man. Oil on canvas, Prague, 1780s. /From the cycle of Prague Burial Society paintings/

Italian Kabbalist Rabbi Aaron Berekhya ben Moses of Modena (d. 1639). In the 18th century, the burial societies would often commission costly illuminated manuscripts of this particular work. Those who are suffering are also remembered in the synagogue divine service, especially during the reading from the Torah, to which it is customary to call a relative or friend of the person who is ill. After the reading, the cantor recites a special blessing for complete recovery – *mi she-berakh le-hole*.

MEDICINE IN THE GHETTO

Sickness represents both divine visitation and a call to help one's fellow beings. This is why medical intervention to heal the sick is not seen as a negation of the will of God but as a religious duty. It is symptomatic that there were many excellent physicians among Jewish religious authorities of the Middle Ages. The most renowned of these was Moses ben Maimon – Maimonides. The medical profession was always highly respected in the Czech lands, although admission was extremely difficult. Because the local universities were not open to Jews until after the reforms of Josef II (1780 – 1790), those who wanted to study medicine had to go abroad. Most frequently they went to the University of Padua and, from the eighteenth century, the universities of Frankfurt-on-Oder and Halle. Of

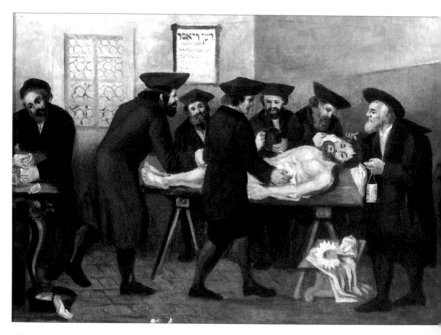

76) Apothecary's Privilege. Manuscript on parchment, pen-and-ink drawing, Vienna, 1783. /Issued by Josef II for Hirschl Michl Jaiteles/

the most prominent Jewish physicians in Prague were the following: in the 16th century Abba Mari Halfan, in the 17th century Aaron Maor Katan Lucerna, Josef Solomon Delmedigo, Menahem ben Asher Mazaretto, Issachar Beer and Judah Leib Teller, in the 18th century Zalman and Moses Gumpertz, Meshullam Bondi, Abraham Kisch and Jonah Jeiteles. The families of Kisch and Jeiteles (Jaiteles) were also involved in pharmacy. Barber-surgeons and midwives played an important role as well in caring for the health of those living in the ghetto.

77) Anonymous Artist, Washing the Body. Oil on canvas, Prague, 1780s. /From the cycle of Prague Burial Society paintings/

DEATH – RITUAL WASHING AND DRESSING OF THE DECEASED

If it is clear that someone is close to death, members of the burial society remain with him or her to the end. It is important to hear the dying person's confession of sins (*vidduy*). As his or her last words, the dying person recites the prayer *Shema Yisrael*. After death, the body is covered in a sheet and laid on the floor, and a candle is lit by his head. In accordance to Jewish law, burial must take place as soon as possible, preferably on the day of death. Once they are informed of the death, members of the burial society dig a grave, make a simple coffin of unplaned boards, and prepare the shroud. The most significant act is the ritual washing of the body (*taharah*). On principle, the male dead is washed by men and the female by women. Taharah is carried out on a stone table or a wooden board. The body is cleansed with warm water into which an egg is mixed as a symbol of life. During the purification, it is necessary to remove all dirt from behind the finger nails – special silver cleaners are used for this purpose. The combs used for arranging the hair of the deceased are also usually made of silver. After the body has been washed, it is then sprinkled with wine. The purification is accompanied by a prayer composed of biblical verses. Once the body has been cleansed and dried, it is then dressed in underwear, a shirt, socks and a shroud (*kittel*) which is held together with a belt. All the above garments, together known as *takhrikhin*, are made of white linen. The male body is, in addition, wrapped in a prayer shawl from which one of the fringes has been removed. The body is placed in the coffin and is sprinkled with soil from the Holy Land. Judaism forbids the placing of jewels and ornaments in the coffin. There must be no difference between the shrouds of the poor and those of the rich. The prayers and acts connected with preparing the body for burial all express faith in resurrection.

אָ

וּדְאעֶר מֵעֶבֶר יַקְּמֵץ
אַחֲרֵי
הַמָּנוֹחַ ה' בְּנִימַן וָאָף
בִּיזְעֶנְץ ז"ל · וְאִשְׁתּוֹ
הַצְּנוּעָה מ' אֶסְתֵּר
נִתְּנָה בְּמַתָּנָה גְּמוּרָה
לְהַגְּעָלֶה ה' יִשְׂרָאֵל
חַיִּים דֵייטְשׁ גַּבַּאי
דִגְמִילוּת חֲסָדִים יַצְ"וּ

78) Kittzur Maavar Yabbok (Maavar Yabbok in an Abridged Version). Manuscript on parchment, ink, tempera, Moravia, 18th century. /Manuscript bequeathed by Benjamin Wolf Bizentz and his wife Esther to the treasurer of the Burial Society/

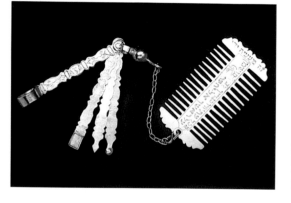

79) Comb and Cleaners. Engraved silver, Moravia, 1770, maker: Moses ben Itzik

The funeral usually starts immediately after the *taharah*. Beforehand, close relatives rend their garments as a sign of mourning. In the first part of the service, known as *Tzidduk ha-Din* (Justification of the Judgement), the cantor recites a prayer which expresses acknowledgement of the Almighty's righteousness and acquiescence in his judgement. After the prayer, the rabbi delivers a funeral speech (*hesped*) over the coffin. The prayer and sermon used to take place in the open air but are now held in the ceremonial hall of the cemetery. After the speech, the funeral

80) Lid of a Burial Society Beaker. Silver, Mikulov (?), 1724/25

procession lines up – in front of the bier and first in succession is a dignitary of the burial society who carries an alms box. He is followed by the immediate relatives of the deceased. Behind the bier proceed the burial society board and the rabbi, followed by the rest of the mourners – the men in front, the women behind. On the way to the grave, the cantor recites Psalm 91 seven times, which stresses the idea of reliance on God's protection at times of need. After the lowering of the body into the grave and a prayer each guest throws three spadefuls of soil onto the coffin. The final part of the funeral again takes place in the ceremonial hall (less frequently at the graveside). It is here that the funeral guests first recite Psalm 49 (on some days Psalm 16) and then hear the *Kaddish* which is recited by the son or other male relative of the deceased. At the end, all present offer

condolence to the survivors. On leaving, all the funeral guests ritually wash their hands. It is customary for friends and neighbours to invite the mourners to a festive Meal of Recovery.

81) Anonymous Artist, Oration over the Dead. Oil on canvas, Prague, 1780s. /From the cycle of Prague Burial Society paintings/

CHARITY AT THE FUNERAL

82) Alms Container. Chased silver, late 18th century

Charity forms an important part of the activities of the burial societies. The collection and distribution of alms (*tzedaka*) – especially for widows, orphans, poor brides and the sick – extends beyond a mere social function. Alms are important not only for the receiver but for the donor, who thereby fulfils an important religious duty. The spiritual significance

which is attached to alms in Judaism is best illustrated by the saying: *Tzedaka tatzil mi-mavet* – alms (charity) protect from death. One of the most important sources of income for burial societies is the alms collected at funerals. Carrying the alms-box (Heb. *kuppa*, Yiddish *bikse* or *pishke*) during the funeral procession is considered to be a great honour. Alms also used to be collected in the burial societies' alms-boxes on other occasions – such as weddings or circumcision ceremonies.

Alms-boxes of burial societies and synagogues can be divided into two basic groups. The first are plates with handles, while the second are closed receptacles with handles and openings in the lids for coin insertion. These alms-boxes could also be placed on permanent display. Most alms boxes are made of silver, although some are brass.

JEWISH CEMETERIES

83) Alms Box. Engraved silver, 18th century

There are various names for a Jewish cemetery in Hebrew, such as *beit kevarot* (the house of graves), *beit hayyim* (the house of life) and *beit olam* (the house of eternity). The cemetery is a holy place where the dead await resurrection and as such must not be closed down according to Jewish law. If this principle was ever broken in the past, it was always the result of external pressure. Acquiring land to establish or extend a cemetery used to involve bureaucratic obstacles and was very costly. Rural communities often had to establish cemeteries in areas of difficult accessibility. In the cramped conditions of the city ghettos it was necessary to bury one grave on top of the other in order to save precious space. With the heaping up of earth, tombstones of older graves were raised to higher levels. The cemetery is surrounded by protective walls and has a mortuary (where the taharah is usually carried out) and a ceremonial hall. A source of water should be available in the cemetery both for the taharah and for the ritual washing of hands after the ceremony. A lavabo at the entrance to the cemetery is used for the latter.

The earliest surviving Jewish cemeteries in the Czech Lands are to be found in Prague and Kolín, the first being established in the 1430s, the second probably not long after. The very earliest cemeteries, however, were all destroyed in pogroms or on the malicious orders of state authorities. Only a small number of tombstones or tombstone fragments dating from the 13th and 14th centuries have survived. These originate from the destroyed cemeteries in Znojmo, Cheb, Brno and Prague (the oldest Prague cemetery was in Vladislavova Street). There are only a few cemeteries which have tombstones from as early as the 16th and the beginning of the 17th centuries – these have survived in Brandýs nad Labem, Mladá Boleslav, Libochovice, Stráž, Ivančice, Mikulov, Roudnice nad Labem, Tovačov and Uherský Brod. There is an increase in the number of cemeteries in the Czech Lands from the latter half of the 17th century onwards. With the Jewish population moving out of the countryside and into the towns from the end of the 19th century, rural cemeteries gradually fell into disrepair. This trend continued well into the next century, intensifying after the tragedy of the Holocaust. During the Communist era, many cemeteries were quite needlessly closed down, often as a result of the cultural ignorance of local bureaucrats. In many communities, however, Jewish cemeteries were kept in good condition thanks to the care taken by local inhabitants. A total of 330 Jewish cemeteries have been preserved in the Czech Lands.

JEWISH TOMBSTONES, EPITAPHS AND SEPULCHRAL SYMBOLS

A tombstone (*matzevah*) is placed over the grave eleven months after the funeral. The vast majority of preserved monuments placed over graves in Jewish cemeteries are made of stone. In the past, wooden structures were also common, but these decayed as a result of unfavourable weather conditions. The most common type of tombstone in the Czech Lands is the stela – an upright slab. The tops of simple stelae, common from the Gothic era to the 19th century, are either level, semicircular or triangular. Architectural stelae appeared in the Renaissance and Baroque eras with semi-columns or pilasters on the sides and waved tympana on top. From the 17th century another type of monument appeared in this country – the tomb (Heb. *ohel* – tent). Tombs resembling sarcophagi were only erected over the graves of major personages. From the mid-19th century the form of Jewish tombstones began to resemble the type commonly found in Christian cemeteries.

84) Fragments of Jewish Tombstones. Marly limestone, Prague, 14th century (?). Fragments from the closed Jewish cemetery in Vladislavova Street, New Town of Prague. Found in 1997 in the gothic cellar of the House at Řečických, Vodičkova Street 10

A Hebrew tombstone inscription as a rule contains the name of the deceased, the date of death, words of praise and a eulogy. The deceased is usually indicated by his forename linked with the forename of his father, and sometimes by his family name and profession. The name is preceded by a title (e.g., "Mr. Abraham, son of the respected Mr. Samuel Brandeis"). In the case of married women, the name of the husband is stated alongside the name of the father (e.g., "Esther, daughter of Natan and wife of David"). The date consists of the day of the week, the day of the month and the year as according to the Jewish calendar. The praise elevates the good qualities and deeds of the deceased. The most significant formula from the eulogy is "May his soul be bound up in the bond of life". Most of the masculine first names inscribed on tombstones are Hebrew biblical or hypocoristic forms of such names (e.g., Heshil for Joshua). Women's first names are also biblical, alongside which there are also significant words of Germanic and Slavonic origin characterising particular qualities or looks – Gutl (good), Slava (renowned), Sheindl (beautiful). Words depicting nature are also common – e.g., Roza or Rezl (rose) and Feigla (little she-bird). Jewish family names usually originated from forenames (Schmelkes, Perles), from a trade or profession (Goldschmied – goldsmith), from the place of origin (Hořovský, Horowitz) or from characteristics and features of the bearer of the name (Shahor – black).

Symbolic images can often be found on Jewish tombstones. In addition to the symbol of Judaism, the Star of David, there are symbols which signify lineage, name, profession or position. Tombstones indicating Kohen (priest, descendant of Aaron) generally depict blessing

85) Wooden Tomb Structure. Oak, Liteň, 1838. /Monument to Wolf Fischer of Málkov and his wife Reizl/

hands, while the symbol for Levites is a pitcher and basin. The forenames and family names of the dead are often symbolised by images of animals or birds. The most frequently depicted animals denote the names of particular tribes of Israel. This connection is based on poetic similes which appear in the blessings of the forefather Jacob to his descendants. Yehuda is compared to a lion, Naftali to a hind, Benjamin to a wolf, and Efraim to fish. Issachar is traditionally associated with a bear. The depiction of the above animals, however, can also refer to other forenames, most of which have their origin in Hebrew or German words for particular "heraldic" animals. Thus, Löb and Leibl are symbolised by a lion, Tzvi and Hirsch by a deer, Zeev and Wolf by a wolf, Dov and Beer by a bear, Fischl and Karpl by a fish. A pigeon denotes the name Jonah, while a dove denotes the female name Taubl. (The above forenames could become family names). Images of other animals and birds are mostly related to family names – Hahn is symbolised by a cock, Gans by a goose, and Lämmel by a lamb. Symbols of trades or professions are less common in the cemeteries of the Czech Lands. Examples include a lancet for doctors, a mortar for apothecaries, and scissors for tailors. An alms box indicates the honourable position of treasurer (gabbai), while circumcision implements signify a mohel.

MOURNING AND REMEMBRANCE OF THE DEAD

During the period following the funeral, the immediate relatives must observe strictly defined rules of conduct – in the first week they may neither work nor leave their homes and it is customary for them to sit on the floor or on low stools. This, the most intensive period of mourning, is known as *shivah* (seven). The next period is called *shloshim* (thirty), during

86) Winding Yahrzeit Calendar. Framed lithograph with winding mechanism, after 1916. /Anniversary of the death of Elise Liebele Kohn/

which the conditions for observing mourning are lessened. *Shloshim* ends on the thirtieth day after the funeral. The longest period of mourning – a whole year – is observed after the death of one's parents. The Kaddish of Orphans (*Kaddish Yetomin*) is recited for the deceased during everyday synagogue service for a period of eleven months after death. The *Yahrzeit* (i.e., anniversary) is first commemorated a year after the funeral and in the following years on the anniversary of the death. The date of the Yahrzeit is based on the Hebrew calendar. The civil calendar (Common Era) date can be found with the help of various aids, e.g. Yahrzeit tablets and calendars. One of the customs connected with the anniversary is the lighting of a commemorative candle (*ner zikkaron*), which should burn for 24 hours. A fundamental part of the Yahrzeit is the reciting of the Kaddish of Orphans by the son or another male relative. The son is also called up to the Torah (usually on the Sabbath preceding the anniversary).

Before the scroll is returned to the Holy Ark following the reading, the *hazzan* (cantor) chants the prayer for the dead *El Male Rahamim* (God Full of Mercy). Along with the Kaddish of Orphans, this prayer is also recited on other occasions – at the unveiling of the tombstone and during the commemorative service, known as *Mazkir* or *Hazkarat Nefashot* (Commemoration of Souls). This service takes place on the Day of Atonement and, in the Ashkenazi region, also on the last days of the Pilgrim Festivals. Respect for late relatives is shown by visiting their graves not just on the Yahrzeit and on the eve of the High Holidays but also during days of public fasting, especially on 9th of Av. As well as on the above dates, it is also customary to visit the graves of saints on 7th of Adar (the anniversary of the death of Moses) and on other special days of burial society fasting (in Prague on the eve of the new moon *Shevat* – usually in January).

87) Anonymous Artist, Annual Prayer at the Grave of Rabbi Loew. Oil on canvas, Prague, ca. 1835. /From the cycle of Prague Burial Society paintings/

THE OLD JEWISH CEMETERY AS DEPICTED BY PRAGUE PAINTERS

The romantic atmosphere of the Old Jewish Cemetery has attracted artists for over two hundred years. Of the numerous works inspired by this cemetery we exhibit graphic art by Karl Würbs, Václav Popelík, Leopold Richter and Bedřich Havránek, drawings by Karl Liebscher and Heinrich Jakesch and paintings by Jan Minařík and a late 18th century anonymous artist.

BURIAL SOCIETY ORGANISATION

The organisational structure and functions of burial societies are defined in the Statutes (*takkanot*). Various associations were affiliated

88) Anonymous Artist, Entrance to the Old Jewish Cemetery between the Klausen Synagogue and the Mortuary. Oil on wood, Prague, late 18th century

to the burial societies, such as the Society of Pious Women (*nashim tzidkoniyot*). Acquiring membership in burial societies was a highly selective process – members were chosen on the basis of their moral qualities and knowledge. They started as candidates and were only accepted as permanent members (*hatumim*) after a several-year waiting period and a public testing of their knowledge. In the Prague Burial Society, an elite group of elders (*zekenim, Altmäner*) was selected from the permanent members who had served for at least fifteen years. Burial society affairs were managed by a board – in smaller communities usually consisting of three members, in Prague of ten. The board was headed by the first representative (*gabbai rishon*) or the *primas*. In Prague the *primas* mainly represented the society before the authorities. The management of internal mat-

89) Jan Minařík, Old Jewish Cemetery and the Tombstone of Rabbi Loew. Oil on canvas, 1899

90) Statutes of the Prague Burial Society. Manuscript on parchment, Prague, 1759, scribe: Gabriel ben Moses Altschul, secretary to the Prague Burial Society. /The document contains transcripts of early statutes (takannot) from the years 1564, 1689, 1692, 1694, 1713, 1717/

91) Statutes of the Prostějov (Prossnitz) Burial Society. Manuscript on parchment, tempera, Prostějov, 1825, scribe: Michael, secretary to the Prostějov Burial Society. The manuscript contains transcripts of documents from 1718

ters, including treasury administration and the distribution of alms, was the responsibility of the *parnas ha-hodesh* (monthly representative). All board members took turns in this position. Although the burial society had a paid sexton (as well as a secretary in larger communities) most of the tasks connected with funerals and management and upkeep of the cemetery were carried out by society members themselves. On principle they received no fees for their services.

The electoral system in the burial society was rather complicated. In smaller societies a newly appointed regular member was also entitled to take part in board elections. He himself could usually only be elected after 4 – 6 years of membership. In Prague, only the elders were allowed to vote. The right to be elected was acquired by Prague elders after a further 3 years of service. Board elections were held each year, in Prague always after the Shavuoth festival. At first, a body of electors from members with voting rights was elected or selected by lot. This group then elected the representatives. In Prague the number of electors was 15, in smaller communities it was mostly 5. One or two proxies were also appointed along with the electors. The first stage of each electoral round was the drawing of lots for the right to nominate a candidate for the board. The elector who gained this right was the one who drew a golden ball. The submitted proposal was then voted for by secret ballot – either

92) Ballot Box. Wood, velvet, silver, Mikulov (Nikolsburg), mid-18th century

a white ball (signifying yes) or a black ball (signifying no) was put into the ballot box (Heb. *kalpe*). An absolute majority was required for a candidate to be elected. This procedure was repeated until the prescribed number of board members was elected. An elector who was also a nominated candidate was not allowed to vote for himself. Instead, a proxy (*nikhnas*) would vote in the relevant round. The same procedure was used if any of the electors were related to the candidate.

ANNUAL BURIAL SOCIETY BANQUET

In carrying out their duties, burial society members had to deal with the tragic side of life. This is why the statutes counted on at least one joyful event in the year – the annual banquet (*seudah shel hevrah kaddisha*). In Prague this was held on the eve of the new month Tammuz (mostly in June). In provincial societies it was often held during the half-holidays of the Pesah. In smaller communities the banquets were attended by all regular members, in larger communities, such as in Prague, only by board members, the group of electors and newly elected members. The banquet retained certain customs common at anniversary guild meetings – especially the drinking from a common jug or beaker.

93) Anonymous Artist, Annual Banquet of the Burial Society. Oil on canvas, Prague, ca. 1835. /From the cycle of Prague Burial Society paintings/

94) Burial Society Beaker. Painted glass, Bohemia, 1787. /From the property of the Prague Burial Society/

95) Burial Society Beaker. Faience, Prague, 1798. /Donated by Hirsch Brandes to the Prague Burial Society

The burial society was a respected and wealthy organisation which did not neglect its public presentation. Some of the rural societies followed the guild custom of commissioning banners which they would march behind at local festivities. Prestige was mostly reflected, however, by the cost and artistic value of objects possessed by the *hevrah kaddisha*. In addition to alms boxes and utensils used during the annual banquet, these were principally silver Torah appurtenances and costly synagogue textiles. The *hevrah* kept Torah appurtenances and curtains in a locked case (*tevah*). These items were only used during divine service on certain occasions – above all on days when commemorative services were being held. A unique way of presentation was the commissioning of pictures depicting activities of the Prague Burial Society. The earliest pictures – portraits of re-

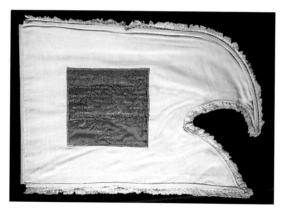

96) Banner of the Society for Visiting the Sick. Silk, appliqué, Bohemia, 1818. /Donated by Daniel Schinder on the birth of his son Anshel/

presentatives – date from the years 1772 – 73. Nothing is known about the painter of these portraits, of which eight have been preserved. The same artist produced the first fifteen pictures from the cycle of Prague Burial Society paintings which date from the 1780s. The paintings document the period when the Old Jewish Cemetery was last used for burials. The idea for both groups of paintings was apparently that of the celebrated Enlightenment physician, Jonah Jeiteles (1735-1806). Four more paintings were added to the cycle in the first half of the 19th century.

CEREMONIAL HALL OF THE BURIAL SOCIETY

The Ceremonial Hall of the Prague Burial Society was built around 1906-1908 in Neo-Romanesque style by the architect Jan Gerstel. The building stands on the site of an earlier mortuary of the Old Jewish Cemetery. The original mortuary is depicted in a late-18th century anonymous painting presented in this Catalogue (No. 88).

97) Anonymous Artist, The Burial Society Board of Trustees. Oil on canvas, 1780s. /From the cycle of Prague Burial Society paintings/

(Arch.= Archive shelf number, Gen. = Genizah, Inv. = Inventory number,
MS = Manuscript, Sg. = Library shelf number, s.n. = without number)

1) Inv. 27.392
2) Inv. 170.193 (MS 34)
3) Sg. 30.149
4) Inv. 8.369/2
   Inv. 17.137 b
   Inv. 17.118
5) Inv. 176.908
   Inv. 176.909
6) Inv. 95.774/2
7) Inv. 23.728 a,b
8) Inv. 3.935
9) Sg. 64.981
10) Inv. 56.831
11) Inv. 17.348
    Inv. 10.984
    Inv. 10.965
    Inv. 3.591
12) Inv. 1432/95
    Inv. 1433/95
13) Inv. 27.795
14) Inv. 12.771
15) Inv. 168.462 (MS 245)
16) Inv. 74.250
17) Inv. 104.785
18) Inv. 173.118
19) Inv. 3.466
20) Inv. 174.839
21) Sg. 5.376
22) Sg. 29.403
23) Inv. 60.768
24) Inv. 61.093
25) Inv. 173.826
26) Inv.168.460 (MS 45)
27) Sg. 65.591
28) Inv. 8.375 a
29) Inv. 164/73

30) Inv. 12.813 b
31) Inv. 52.185
32) Inv. 44.437
33) Inv. 148/95
34) Inv. 24.433/67
    (MS 313)
35) Inv.174.253
36) Inv. 21/82 a,b
37) Inv. 125.572
38) Inv. 61.383
39) Inv. 66.125
40) Sg. 29.703
41) Inv. 3.432 a
42) Inv. 27.376
43) Inv. 2.964
44) Inv. 17.111
45) Inv. 17.376
46) Gen. Luže Inv.1
47) Inv. 17.720
48) Inv. 173.930
49) Inv. 32.141
50) Inv. 12.785
51) Inv. 170.565 (MS 243)
52) Inv. 174.932
53) Inv. 32.893
54) Inv. 5.950
55) Inv. 32.132
56) Inv. 46.491
57) Inv. 97.371
58) Inv. 33/72
59) Inv. 170.173 (MS 10)
60) Inv. 5.185
61) Inv.173.648
62) Inv. 3.993
63) Inv. 49.422
64) –

65) –
66) Inv. 61.943
67) Inv. 66.479
68) Inv. 23.926
69) Inv. 1.395
70) Inv. 175.895
71) Inv. 91.922 a
    Inv. 2.472/2
72) Inv. 7.580
73) Inv. 31.801
74) Inv. 3.176 (MS 241)
75) Inv. 12.843/1
76) Arch. 32.330
77) Inv. 12.843/5
78) Inv. 170.566 (MS 244)
79) Inv. 4.520
80) Inv. 3.941
81) Inv. 12.843/9
82) Inv. 2.211
83) Inv. 48.529
84) s.n.
85) Inv. 173.614
86) Inv. 537/95
87) Inv. 12.843/16
88) Inv. 27.007
89) Inv. 118.506
90) Arch. 42.842
91) Inv. 170.217 (MS 65)
92) Inv. 4.526
93) Inv. 12.843/17
94) Inv. 63.619
95) Inv. 63.621
96) Inv. 2.079
97) Inv. 12.843/15

JEWISH CUSTOMS AND TRADITIONS
FESTIVALS, THE SYNAGOGUE
AND THE COURSE OF LIFE

(EXHIBITION GUIDE)

Text: PhDr. Alexandr Putík
Translation: Joy Moss Kohoutová, Stephen Hattersley
Selection of photographs: PhDr. Eva Kosáková
Photographs: Dana Cabanová
Drawings: Hana Pavlátová
Editor: PhDr. Alexandr Putík
Layout: Aleš Krejča
Published by the Jewish Museum in Prague, 1998
Reprint 2002
Printed by Label, Kutná Hora

ISBN 80-85608-23-5

THE JEWISH MUSEUM IN PRAGUE
U Staré školy 1,3, 110 01 Praha 1
http://www.jewishmuseum.cz
Bank account No.:
195420830257 / 0100 (US Dollars)
510091870297 / 0100 (Euro)
Komerční banka,
Spálená 51, 110 00 Praha 1